Upheaval

Navid Kermani

Upheaval

The Refugee Trek through Europe

With photography by Moises Saman

Translated by Tony Crawford

polity

First published in German as *Einbruch der Wirklichkeit: Auf dem Flüchtlingstreck durch Europa* © Verlag C.H. Beck oHG, Munich, 2016

This English edition © Polity Press, 2017

Photography © Moises Saman/Magnum Photos
Map © Peter Palm, Berlin/Germany

Polity Press
65 Bridge Street
Cambridge CB2 1UR, UK

Polity Press
350 Main Street
Malden, MA 02148, USA

ISBN-13: 978-1-5095-1867-8
ISBN-13: 978-1-5095-1868-5 (pb)

A catalogue record for this book is available from the British Library.

Typeset in 12/16pt Janson Text LT Std
by Servis Filmsetting Ltd, Stockport, Cheshire
Printed and bound in the UK by CPI Group (UK) Ltd, Croydon

The publisher has used its best endeavours to ensure that the URLs for external websites referred to in this book are correct and active at the time of going to press. However, the publisher has no responsibility for the websites and can make no guarantee that a site will remain live or that the content is or will remain appropriate.

For further information on Polity, visit our website: politybooks.com

Acknowledgements

From 24 September to 2 October 2015, Moises Saman and I travelled from Budapest to Izmir on assignment for the German news weekly *Der Spiegel*. A much shorter version of our report – about a third of the present text – appeared in the 11 October issue. I owe thanks to many people: Lothar Gorris, head of the magazine's cultural section, Matthew Krug, photography editor, and Gordon Bertsch of *Der Spiegel*'s travel office all gave us the best support possible. Alex Stathopoulos of Pro Asyl, Ramona Lenz and Thomas Gebauer of medico international, and Hagen Knopp of Watch the Med helped us plan our route and put us in touch with people along the way. Başak Demir helped me prepare for the visit to Turkey. Nicole Courtney-Leaver got us the necessary credentials and was very helpful in many other matters. My assistant Florian Bigge kept us supplied during the trip with current information and situation reports from Germany. The writer Vladimir Arsenijević and the cultural manager Milena Berić of Belgrade picked us up at the Hungarian–Serbian border and accompanied us as far as Thessaloniki Airport. Vladimir and Milena were much more than our drivers, interpreters and guides: they gave us the invaluable gifts of their insights, their inexhaustible contacts throughout the Balkan region, and most of all their friendship. Finally, I thank my editor at C. H. Beck, Dr Ulrich Nolte, and his assistant Gisela Muhn, who supervised the book version.

Immediately after we left Lesbos, my brother Khalil and my sister-in-law Bita arrived there and initiated an aid project for the refugees. See http://avicenna-hilfswerk.de/avicenna-english/ to find out more or to donate.

Navid Kermani
Cologne, 10 December 2015

A Strangely Softer Germany

It was a strangely softer Germany that I left in late September 2015. In the railway stations of the big cities, between the travellers hurrying to their trains or their exits, strangers lay on green foam mats. No one chased them away or caused a fuss about the public disorder; on the contrary, local residents in yellow safety vests knelt beside the strangers to offer them tea and sandwiches or to play with their children. Outside the stations were tents and people going into them, carrying box after box – food, clothing, toys, medicines – donations from the populace. When other countries stopped the strangers and bullied them so badly that they tried to escape on foot along the motorways, Germany sent special trains to fetch them, and, wherever they arrived, crowds of citizens and even mayors were on the platforms to applaud them. Local newspapers and national TV networks alike told their audiences what every single German could do to help, and overnight even the most xenophobic of the German papers began recounting the strangers' life stories, telling so compellingly of war, of oppression, and of the travails and dangers of their flight that it was impossible, even in the pubs, to think rescuing them a bad idea. In the towns and villages, citizens' committees formed – not against the new neighbours, but *for* them. The football clubs in the national league – the Bundesliga – sewed patches on their jerseys saying refugees were welcome, and the most popular actors and singers inveighed against all Germans who did not show solidarity.

Yes, there was also animosity against the strangers, there were attacks, but now the politicians leapt to the defence of the threatened refugees and visited their shelters. The chancellor herself, the hard-headed German chancellor who, just a few weeks before, had been helpless to comfort a weeping girl from Palestine, amazed everyone by an outburst of emotion as she defended the right to political asylum. Her whole government, for that matter: was this the same government that, a few months earlier, had been the loudest critic of Italy's Mare Nostrum project to save boat refugees from drowning? And the state, the German administration: to provide for hundreds of thousands of new refugees within a few weeks exceeded any foreseeable contingency, and yet it was managed surprisingly well. At most there was discreet grumbling about schools being unable to use their sports halls, about furtive estimates of the costs, which might entail new debt. And what if another million refugees were to come next year, and still more the year after?

It was a strangely softer Germany I left behind, as if its greyness, usually so stiff and forbidding, was covered with powdered sugar. Just as I was leaving, I couldn't help thinking, or perhaps I already felt, how easily powdered sugar can be blown away.

A Great Migration

From the veranda of my hotel on Lesbos, I can see the Turkish coast a few kilometres away across the Mediterranean Sea. It is half past eight in the morning, and right now, as I write this sentence, the first group of refugees is coming round the bend in the lane below – all of them Afghans, from their appearance and the snatches I can hear of their talk, and all men; their inflatable boat has apparently landed in Europe without major difficulties. They do not look drenched or frozen, as many other refugees do who land, for fear of the police, below cliffs or steep, overgrown slopes, or who make the crossing in boats that are desperately overcrowded. Now that they have survived the most dangerous part of their long journey, they are cheerful, positively chipper; they're

➤ FOLLOWING PAGES:
Miratovac, Serbia: refugees who have marched from Macedonia to Serbia, avoiding the border stations.

talking and joking, looking like a group of young day-trippers, carrying nothing but hand luggage at most. They don't know yet, though, that they have a steeply climbing march of several kilometres ahead of them to get to one of the buses that the United Nations refugee agency has chartered to take new arrivals to the port of Mytilene; nor have they any inkling that, because the United Nations doesn't have enough buses, most of the refugees have to walk the fifty-five kilometres to the port, with no food, no sleeping bags, no warm clothes – and the sun is still glaring during the day, while the nights have grown chilly.

There are aircraft that fly faster than sound and ships like floating holiday resorts; there are trains as comfortable as living rooms and coaches with kitchens, baths and reclining armchairs; there are taxis with wireless Internet access and soon there will be self-driving cars – but the refugees, in the year 2015, are marching through Europe like the people of Israel fleeing from Egypt. In films and paintings of biblical scenes, you always see a great throng of people with their prophet leading the way. As we drove from Mytilene to the north coast, I saw the shape great migrations really take: a long, seemingly endless string of small and tiny groups, at different intervals and in varying formations, now in single file, now three or four abreast. The groups seem to be united by nothing except their destination. Even those who come from the same country are usually from different cities and regions. And within the small groups, too, the people are often strangers, chance acquaintances now sharing a common destiny. At first the whole group of forty or fifty who sat together in one boat stay together, but on the first uphill stretch, not a hundred yards past my hotel, the young, single men take the lead and the families fall behind.

These are Europe's bogeymen: the single men bound for Europe, ominously referred to as 'young Muslim men!' in talk shows and letters to the editor. Their appearance does not betray whether they are actually religious: hardly any of them wears a beard; no one is wearing traditional garb; nowhere do they stop for communal prayer. In fact, considering their situation – when was the last time they were able to shower, when did they last sleep in a bed? – the men are remarkably clean-shaven. That alone would be a sign of defiance in the Islamic dictatorships, and maybe that's what it is: after all, many of the Syrians, Iraqis and Afghans have fled from a situation in which shaving is punishable by death. But it's true that men make up the vast majority of the refugees, and most of them are young – eighteen, twenty, twenty-five. Perhaps there's a simple reason for that, though – one that is immediately obvious on Lesbos: young men are best suited to endure the difficulties, the dangers, the sheer physical exertion that is required to apply for asylum in Europe. By forcing all the refugees to board the inflatable boats and then march for days on foot, European asylum laws unintentionally select the physically strong, and also the spartan, in other words the poor, who are not accustomed to middle-class comforts to begin with. Fifty-five kilometres is a long way, especially if you are already exhausted or famished on setting out and have no decent shoes, no warm clothes, no provisions – then fifty-five kilometres goes on for-ever. And every car that passes by the refugees with its back seat empty, I assume, must become an object of hatred. But a simple bottle of water handed out of the window, I discovered on my way to the north coast, becomes a gift from Heaven.

Do We Want Europe or Don't We?

When I arrived in Budapest, the capital of the European country known for its xenophobia, I was surprised not to see any foreigners at all. Of course the city centre was populated by the same tourists who overrun Prague, London or Berlin; by foreign-ers I mean people who had immigrated or fled to

Hungary. And as I rode the metro outwards from the city centre, the faces in the trains remained white and I heard no other language besides the indigenous one. There is not a single refugee in sight even in John Paul II Park, where in August the thousands whose flight along the motorway inspired the German chancellor to open the border had been stranded. The homogeneity is even odder when you consider the fact that, up until the Second World War, Budapest was a – if not *the* – multicultural metropolis of Europe, and until 300 years ago the seat of an Ottoman vizier. The Turkish baths are still an obligatory stop on any tourist visit to the city.

I had an appointment to meet Júlia, Eva and Stefan, three of the many volunteers who had cared for the refugees in the park. It was odd: one of them told me her real name only when we met face to face; another didn't answer the telephone at all but texted me first to ask who was calling. Purely a precaution, they said, and were surprised that I was surprised: after all, they were aiding illegal aliens. As recently as July they had been leading ordinary lives as a translator, a psychologist, a financial advisor, couldn't have imagined that they would one day become activists, weren't even particularly political. But then, in early August, they were confronted with the misery on their very doorstep and talked to the refugees, who were neither

➤ FOLLOWING PAGES:
Opatovac, Croatia: after registration, refugees board a bus that will take them from the Serbian border to a train to Hungary.

freeloaders nor terrorists, the allegations on television notwithstanding, but ordinary people like themselves, among them translators, psychologists and financial advisors. Through Facebook they joined together in activist groups that formed within hours. Except for the very sporadic deliveries of the Red Cross and other organizations, the sustenance of thousands of refugees depended for many weeks on the work and donations of the inhabitants of Budapest.

The state did not merely fail to help: through its media it heaped contempt on the volunteers, claiming they were being paid by George Soros, thus pandering to the old anti-Semitic resentment while at the same time spreading propaganda against Muslims. Along the streets, government billboards showed a blonde beauty proclaiming she objected to illegal aliens – after the government had practically declared that all refugees who did not enter the country legally were criminals. Other posters explained to foreigners that they must respect Hungarian culture, once in Hungary they must speak Hungarian – explained it to them in Hungarian, in fact, so that the posters can hardly have been intended for the foreigners; their audience was the government's own voters. There are racists everywhere, but racism in Hungary is drilled into people by the state itself. That a camerawoman trips a Syrian carrying his child – no: that she does so shamelessly, in front of other cameras – is a result of the constant, systematic defamation of the refugees, and everything foreign, in the discourse of Hungarian politics and media.

The government's campaign against refugees forged strong bonds between the volunteers, who continued to meet even though there were no more refugees in Budapest. Once a person has been deeply moved, touched by real encounters with human beings, they can't forget the issue, explained Eva, the psychologist, a blonde-haired forty-something in an elegant red dress. Whatever she might have done, the refugees had repaid her with their gratitude and with the insights they offered into unknown worlds. By now, Eva laughed, she's a regular Middle East expert. Instead of Hungarian television she now watches CNN and the English-language Al Jazeera channel. But Eva also talked about how isolated she feels: she can no longer talk to some of her acquaintances at all; even the more common remarks about refugees now sound too offensive to her. 'When someone gets nasty with me on Facebook, I just block them.'

Eva knows she belongs to a minority in Hungary, a minority that is large in Budapest, and growing, but in the countryside, she said, hardly anyone thinks as she does. The government intentionally left the refugees in the parks and the railway stations, with no way to take care of themselves, to make them look degenerate, she says, to make them stink, so that people would be afraid of them, especially of the young men at night. When she took a Syrian family into her home, a family who had walked for three days, even her own sixteen-year-old son grumbled; he checked whether they had stolen anything.

Györgi Dragomán, who in his early forties is already one of the country's most renowned writers, joined us in the café. 'Yes, that's true,' he concurred with Eva, who was telling me more about her alienation from her own society, 'I'm living in a bubble too.' The surveys claim that seventy per cent of Hungarians supported the government's refugee policy, but, he said, he doesn't know anyone among the seventy per cent. All his acquaintances and all the writers despise the current government. It isn't good to talk only to like-minded people, but Hungarian society is totally divided; people no longer come together, if only to disagree, even on public platforms. And what would they discuss, anyway? The talk about the Christian Occident is a farce, he says; until recently the government had no interest at all in Christianity, referred rather to the pagan traditions of a Greater Hungary and even advocated an Eastern opening, towards the allegedly related Turkish peoples, to loosen ties with the EU. The still more extreme right wing, he continued, has always supported the Palestinians in the Middle East and maintained good relations with Hamas. Now Victor Orbán is suddenly concerned about women's rights – he who has not a single female minister in his cabinet. He is exploiting the refugee crisis to promote his notion of homogeneous nations by fomenting xenophobia all over Europe. Ultimately, Györgi Dragomán said, the question is, do we want Europe or don't we? The enemy in Hungary is ostensibly Muslims, he said, but in fact it is every form of deviation, difference per se: homosexuality, Jews, Roma, critical media, opposition.

Has he ever thought of applying for political asylum in another country himself? I asked jokingly.

'When they start censoring my books, I will leave Hungary,' Györgi Dragomán answered.

Why Are You All Coming Here?

As I write this, another group of Afghans is walking past my hotel, only this time there is a young, unveiled woman in jeans among them, doubtless a city-dweller. That is unusual. As I travelled across the Balkans to Lesbos, almost all the Afghans I met coming the other way were from rural areas, spoke no

---

➤ FOLLOWING PAGES:
Opatovac, Croatia: refugees waiting to be registered outside the reception camp.

other language besides Dari, and were visibly not the skilled workers and engineers that German businesses are hoping for.

'Why are you all coming here?' I asked yesterday as I gave at least the old people, women and children a lift in my car, nine or ten people at a time packed as tightly as possible into the little jeep, 'What do you think you'll find in Germany?'

'Work,' they answered, 'school, a little safety: there's no future in Afghanistan.'

'And why is everyone coming now?' I asked further, pointing out that there had been no future in Afghanistan last year either.

'They said on television Germany is accepting refugees,' they explained time after time when I asked why they had set out in early September, 'and we saw the pictures of the German train stations.'

Most of them sold their possessions and made their way to Iran, then continued on foot over the mountains to Turkey, doing without shelter and hot meals to save money; they hired smugglers in Izmir, who in some cases took from them more than the agreed price of 1,200 euros; once at sea many found their boat overloaded and had to throw all their baggage overboard, and then wondered, on arriving in Lesbos, how they were supposed to get to Germany empty-handed, or with all their money gone. Shit, I thought, this is not how the 'welcoming culture' was supposed to play out.

'And now?'

They need 65 euros for the ferry to Piraeus, I explained to them, 40 euros for the bus to the Macedonian border, the train through Macedonia is free, 35 euros for the bus through Serbia, then free trains and buses again via Croatia, Hungary, Austria to Germany. With luck they'll manage to sleep somehow. At the borders the aid agencies have set up tents, although there aren't enough for everyone; at least from Macedonia on they'll get a little food and things like nappies. And, yes, the borders are open at the moment – for how long, no one knows.

'But whatever you do, don't tell your relatives at home to set out after you,' I always added. 'Since when do you believe what they say on television?'

The next group is already approaching, the sixth in less than two hours, another forty, fifty refugees who sat jammed together on an inflatable boat, whole families among them this time, even babies. Some of this group are carrying the shiny gold and silver thermal blankets that crackle in the wind, so apparently they arrived soaked and were attended to by the aid volunteers who wait for the boats on the north coast of Lesbos. I ought to be jumping up and giving at least the mothers, children and old people a lift up the hill to the bus stop. The young men will have to walk another fifty kilometres to the port anyway, where they will camp in a car park until they can get a seat on the ferry to Piraeus, assuming they have 65 euros for the ticket.

The European Border Regime

Because Hungary had closed its border with Serbia to refugees, we went from Budapest to Šid on the Serbian border with Croatia. When we arrived at the little border post, Croatia had just allowed the refugees to enter, after they had been stuck waiting for days in a cemetery between the two countries' border stations. Before and between the tombstones, we saw what they had left lying: ordinary camping tents that volunteers had provided, nappies, water bottles, Christian missionaries' pamphlets in various languages, empty tins, blankets, plenty of rubbish where bins were lacking. A few kilometres further west, the regular European border regime was restored: the Croatian police collected the refugees in prison vans and drove them to a camp near the town of Opatovac. They didn't look annoyed on arriving there; they seemed relieved to be moving at all. Even while queuing to be registered, which took hours, they didn't complain. In spite of the adversity of the situation – a makeshift camp of army tents, much too small for several thousand refugees, in the middle of a field in the chill autumn wind – the mood was almost businesslike: never a raised voice; now and then a smile, in fact. Aid workers cheered up the children where necessary.

By chance I interviewed the Croatian home minister, Ranko Ostojić, who had got out of his official car in hiking trousers, as if he too was about to march to Germany. Three or four Croatian journalists had been informed about his visit here, but no one had notified the international press, so I was taken, unasked, to see the minister. The minister assured me that Croatia treated the refugees properly – I was welcome to observe all operations and form my own opinion – there were camp beds, sufficient food, doctors and even showers. He was especially proud that no refugee would stay in Croatia for more than twenty-four hours. As soon as they had been registered, the refugees would be taken, if transport capacities permitted, to the nearest railway station, where special trains would take them to Hungary. To Hungary? Yes, to Hungary: that is another oddity in these European times. Hungary boasts of defending the border to Serbia with fences and barbed wire against the onslaught of refugees and tacitly lets those same refugees enter via Croatia, provided they immediately travel on to Austria; the Hungarian state even assists them with free buses. Naturally that makes a mockery of Europe as a mutually supportive community; however, those who complain about other countries unloading refugees by opening wide their exits may be reminded that Germany too resisted cries for fair distribution as long as it was Greeks or Italians who were bearing the heaviest burden. The refugee crisis started long before Germany became conscious of it.

I asked the Croatian home minister what would happen if the Germans closed their border.

'They can't,' the minister answered.

'What do you mean, they can't?'

'You can't stop people who are that desperate. If they don't get through in one place, they'll find another. And if you build walls, they'll sit there in front of the wall until we can't stand to look at them. Ultimately, the only way to stop refugees is by shooting at them. No one wants that.'

Of course it strains Germany to take in more than a million refugees in one year, and in many areas the strain is too great. The affluent neighbourhoods and cities may find it easier to support them, but places that are already groaning under unemployment and social conflicts may well grumble when still more destitute people need to be helped, more foreigners need to be absorbed. At the same time, though, we must realize what would happen, or is already happening in some places, if we respond with rigour and isolation. Our own hearts would harden, and the openness that constitutes Europe as a project and a product of the Enlightenment would wither. We would see tremendous misery, not outside Europe's borders, but right at the borders of Germany, while we refused to reach out our hands. To do that, though, we must demonize the others, blame them for their own fate – blame their culture, race or religion – denigrate them in books, in the media and ultimately on billboards, always emphasize the bad things about them and so make them into barbarians to keep their suffering at arm's length. Do we want Europe or don't we?

It is no coincidence that the photo of a drowned child, more than anything else, was what penetrated the public awareness and broke through the barriers to compassion. Children escape the mechanisms of public contempt because they can hardly be blamed for their fate. You would have to have laced up your heart very tight indeed not to take pity on a child. It can be done, but it can't be done without crippling your whole personality. Everyone saw on television how uneasy the chancellor looked – you could see just by the clumsy gesture of her caress that she was

➤ FOLLOWING PAGES:
Opatovac, Croatia: Afghan refugees waiting to be let out of a prison van before registration in the camp.

physically uncomfortable – because she couldn't give the crying Palestinian girl any other answer than the correct one: that not all refugees are admitted. The chancellor looked so much more composed weeks later in a selfie taken with refugees, looks surprisingly relaxed in her interviews too since she has begun advocating Germany's openness, evidently a matter close to her heart. It feels good to do good. I feel good too when I file my reports: one comfort more as I go on leading my life of affluence.

At Opatovac the refugees were let out of the prison vans only when the queue in front of the registration office had shortened somewhat. They often waited in the vans for half an hour, sometimes a whole hour, behind bars, and yet they were better off than if they had had to stand in the open in the chill evening air. Only the children had difficulty waiting in such cramped quarters. The policeman to whom the prison vans were assigned, a well-groomed Croatian of about fifty, silently opened the doors, gave a hand to the elderly or lifted the children down from the van, but never smiled. Only once, a Syrian girl, perhaps five years old, with black shoulder-length hair and a bright, friendly face, brushed the policeman so gently over his blue uniform as he lifted her down, running her open hand from his shoulder almost down to his stomach, as if he were a treasure, that it brought tears to the policeman's eyes. It all happened in less than a second, two at most, but I was standing just three feet away and I saw it clearly, saw the girl's gesture, which surprised me as much as it did him, and the moisture that formed in the policeman's eyes. A moment longer than usual the policeman held the girl on his arm as she beamed back at him with joy. Then he set her down; the girl skipped after her mother to join the queue. As he wiped the tear from his eye, the policeman noticed that I had observed the scene; immediately he looked away, as if I had caught him doing something improper. 'It's nothing to be ashamed of,' I would have liked to call out to him.

Culture Shock

Today I drove down a difficult track to the lighthouse at the northwest point of Lesbos with the photographer Moises Saman, who is accompanying me on this trip. Many boats land here too, yet there are no aid volunteers for miles around. It is a strange, sometimes almost morbid sight when the refugees are embraced willy-nilly on their arrival by long-haired men or scantily clad women wearing yellow safety vests and screaming 'welcome, welcome'. If I were an Afghan, such a strangely warm welcome might make me want to turn right around and go back. But I am judging too harshly. In the face of the Greek state's complete indifference – doesn't Greece have a leftist government? – the aid workers are doing magnificent work on Lesbos, providing warm clothing and the gold and silver emergency blankets, distributing sandwiches and water, and putting up tents if it's too late in the day to travel on. Doctors who have given up their holidays treat the injured and calm those who have been traumatized by the crossing. It is moving, too, to observe how cultures mix among the aid workers: even the Israeli and the Islamic NGOs sit together in the taverna in the evenings. But most of all I am amazed to see that, apart from the few professional aid workers and political activists, those who devote themselves to helping the refugees on Lesbos or at the border stations along the march are almost without exception young people, twenty, twenty-five years old – like many of the refugees themselves – members of a generation that we too readily dismiss as apolitical and self-absorbed. After this crash course in life experience and world politics, they don't need any soap-box speakers to explain to them why Europe is necessary: fear of death and tears of joy, destitution and gratitude, prayers and piercing questions leap towards them out of every boat. The volunteers too live through a boundary experience every time they take and carry a baby carefully up the slippery rocks to the nearest beach, talking calmly to it all the while, pressing the baby to their chest with both arms to comfort and warm it at the same time, until finally the parents arrive beside them, sopping wet, trembling with cold and happiness: the really big emotions inevitably take hold of you, tears, tenderness and always rage against a European asylum policy that imposes this torture, this mortal danger, like a perverse initiation ritual, on those in need of sanctuary. It is just as Eva said, and all the aid workers confirm it: once they have been deeply moved, touched by real encounters with human beings, the young people devoting themselves to the refugees will not so easily forget the distress that exists outside Europe.

And yet a few of the activists, some political ones in particular, display a self-righteousness, a paternalism, towards the refugees, and an aggressive arrogance that occasionally makes one nostalgic for the good old Civil Defence Corps or the Salvation Army. More than once I wondered why so many hands were reaching out to the refugees as they landed, while in the hinterland, where helping is not rewarded with the really big emotions, comparatively few activists are at work. Doing good sometimes does the doer the most good: that too is observable on the north coast of

➤ FOLLOWING PAGES:
Miratovac, Serbia: a refugee child under a rain cape in the no man's land between Macedonia and Serbia.

Lesbos. It doesn't occur to the tattooed and scantily dressed volunteers that their idea of freedom might be different from that of the Afghans and Syrians they press, regardless of sex – 'welcome, welcome' – to their chests.

All right, perhaps the culture shock many refugees experience on landing is at the same time an excellent preparation for the free West, which can sometimes be very strange indeed. And the reporters, who also await the refugees on the north coast in great numbers, and the highly competitive photographers, are not always the epitome of sensitivity, running into the water with their cameras to be the first to reach the boats, and screaming at the aid workers to get out of the picture. In the two days since I arrived on Lesbos, I have seen several scuffles and one real fight between aid workers and photographers. I was bawled out by a camera team myself because I blocked the dirt road for three minutes when I stopped to let soaking-wet women and children climb into the jeep. Of course, not all photographers work so ruthlessly – certainly not Moises, although he too is very determined. That's why he drives to the northwest tip of the island, where no one gets in his way. Yet he can't yield immediately to the impulse to reach out his hand because his task is a different one. In politics too, perhaps, it may not always be right to follow one's first impulse when one wants to help. Often it *is* right – but when? Just imagine what would have happened to the thousands of desperate travellers on the Hungarian motorway – very concretely: where would they have slept, who would have fed them, what kind of force would have been used to stop them at the border? – if Germany had not opened its borders to them. That willingness to offer relief, so unexpected then, has since been transformed, as if in a game of Chinese whispers, into an open invitation that is still being broadcast on Afghan television.

Unfortunately, the wind is blustery today, the sea dotted with whitecaps – or should we be relieved to see a day on which no boats are attempting the crossing? We look out in vain for the red dots that clusters of life vests appear as when spied in the distance. On ordinary days, three and sometimes four thousand refugees land on the north coast, up to a hundred boats, usually within a few hours, on a stretch of coastline just a few kilometres long. Not a single pebble can be seen on the beach right below the lighthouse because it is completely covered with life vests, life-saving rings, inner tubes, and the remains of the inflatable boats. As we look along the coast from here, Lesbos glows for miles with the red and orange of the life vests. But not everything is left on the beach: wherever boats land, a pickup truck soon drives up, and its driver recovers the outboard motor and the rigid plastic floorboard of the inflatable boat. Only the black tubes remain. The refugees assemble in the meantime to move on; the pickup drives off without taking them. That often seems as merciless as the fervour we journalists display to catch the biggest emotions, the best picture, and yet it becomes more understandable with every passing day when you try yourself to go about your business on the island. After all, the locals are not on a temporary assignment, they live here permanently; with time their feelings have been numbed. I notice it happening to me: I can't spend all day driving refugees back and forth or interpreting for them if I want to have time to write, and now I usually drive past them without a second glance.

On the first day, I had a discussion with Moises because I wanted to drive some refugees who were stranded in the middle of nowhere to the port, but he insisted that's not what we're here for. I admitted he was right and climbed into the jeep with my guilty conscience, and without the refugees, and a moment later we landed in a ditch. And what happened then? Without waiting to be asked, the Syrians who had just disembarked from their inflatable boat half an hour earlier lifted our jeep and carried it back onto the

track. Luckily there were enough young men among
them.

In the City Centre

Just as on Lesbos, life in Belgrade goes on, and here
refugees camp in the green spaces in front of the railway station, right in the city centre – formerly green
spaces, to be exact, because the ground now consists of
nothing but bare earth. The evening we arrived, it was
raining torrents and all we could see were the coloured
camping tents growing under the trees like giant mush-
rooms. Then we noticed the tent walls moving here
and there, and deduced that there were people behind
them sitting all packed together. We discovered more
refugees when we looked up at the upper levels of a car
park. They were crouching between the cars, wrapped
in brown blankets. You quickly develop a sensitivity to
changes in the weather when you're fleeing to Europe.
It's not just the wet, not just the cold; it's also the mud,
the dirt, that the rain always brings with it. Where will
they get dry, where will they wash, when will they next
be able to change their clothes? And what will happen
when autumn really sets in?

Since January the refugees have gathered in the
centre of Belgrade, several thousand of them at times,

and that is not counting those who stayed in guest-houses. There are still hundreds camping in front of the station, even though the way to Croatia and from there to Germany is open. These are the poorest, and hence almost all of them are Afghans: they no longer have even the 10 euros for the bus to Šid. They are being supplied with food and clothing by volunteers and the Red Cross; after several months the city government at least provided portable toilets and set up a medical station under a tarpaulin. The state, meanwhile, does nothing, although it would surely be easy enough to provide a lift to the border for a few hundred or even a thousand refugees who want nothing better than to leave anyway. Apparently Serbia has long since grown accustomed to seeing them here. German public opinion would see such a park as the very embodiment of governmental failure, of the deluge of asylum seekers, of apocalyptic chaos, yet when we returned the next morning in sunshine I was surprised to see the shops and cafés open round about, the traffic backing up perfectly normally, the pavements as crowded as ever. The Afghans confirmed that very few Belgraders are hostile towards them. That is of course one way to deal with the refugees: neither demonizing nor caring for them, but simply leaving them to their fate.

At the very edge of one of the parks, half hidden by shrubbery, I saw a boy, hardly sixteen years old, dark-skinned, lying under one of the brown blankets. The boy's hair stuck out wildly as if he had slathered it with gel, and mud covered his face and limbs. His body was racked by chills, and he wheezed heavily in his sleep. But the most frightening thing was his bare feet: there was barely any skin left whole between the calluses, bruises and open blisters. I wondered how far the boy had walked to Belgrade, from what country. And why hadn't he found shelter last night, in a tent or in the car park? Because I took him for a Pashtun, I went and asked the Afghans camping nearby to come with me to where the boy was; maybe they would know what was the matter with him. But no one knew the boy. In the end we shook him awake and took him to the medical station at the other end of the park. When the boy opened his eyes, he seemed so delirious that he probably thought we were all figments of his dreams. Moaning, he spoke a few sentences. Then I realized he was speaking Serbian. The Roma have been fleeing to Serbia for many years.

Autobahn to Germany

I have returned to my place on the veranda and am connecting the stories I've heard with the refugees walking past the hotel – Syrians or Iraqis at the

➤ FOLLOWING PAGES:
Gevgelija, Macedonia: refugees who walked across the fields from Greece enter the Macedonian border town.

moment, many young people this time, men and only veilless women, who would be outwardly indistinguishable from the aid volunteers if they were to put on yellow safety vests. The hairstyles, the brand-name jeans and trainers, the sunglasses and earphones identify them as members of the global middle class; even their rucksacks are the same ones Westerners take when they go hiking. These are not the have-nots who make up the majority of refugees; in Mytilene they will probably spend the money for a hostel instead of sleeping by the docks, and they will make better time through Europe, if only because they speak English and have smartphones. And yet they too, every one of them, have a story to tell that no Western European life can match for drama, suffering and violence: barrel bombs falling on their cities, crucified bodies on display for days, critical theatre plays punished by torture. War is raging on the southern and eastern borders of our enclave of affluence, and every single refugee is a herald of it: they are the irruption of reality into our consciousness.

Those who complete the march to the port without accident will get off a train at a German station in six or seven days. They would never guess how fast they'll travel from Piraeus on, riding a direct bus to the Macedonian border, marching two, three kilometres through no man's land, getting registered, boarding a train that goes straight to the Serbian border, marching through no man's land again, getting registered again and then boarding another bus. The same thing at the Croatian, the Hungarian, the Austrian border, except that from Serbia on they don't have to march across the border; they get a lift. Taken all together, what the European border regime has built for the refugees is an autobahn to Germany. And in fact Germany is where everyone I talked to wanted to go, although some only to continue from there to Scandinavia or to other countries where they have family. To the refugees, the individual stops are hardly distinguishable from one another: of course the officials' uniforms and languages change, but the field camps, the camping tents and the containers stay the same; everywhere the same brown blankets, transparent rain capes and collapsible umbrellas distributed by the United Nations refugee agency, the same police and soldiers, neither rude nor particularly friendly, as if by unified European orders; the same volunteers in their yellow safety vests organizing food, nappies, warmer clothes and adapters to charge phones; the doctors, too, the same everywhere with their stethoscopes, and the Christian missionaries with their pamphlets. And at every improvised border post, and every station where they change trains between Piraeus and Munich, rows of sky-blue portable toilets. Europe is united at least in this: that refugees shall not have to relieve themselves in the open, but in stinking, filthy plastic cubicles, for days and weeks on end. The portable toilets are the hallmark of European humanity.

At every stage of the refugees' route, a little multicultural economy has also taken shape: suddenly Afghan pilaf is on the menu in the remotest Serbian village; a Macedonian coffee house serves tea; in Belgrade the price of a haircut or a bed for the night is advertised in Arabic. Taxi drivers are raising their fares sharply, and where the official fare for the bus ride through Serbia is 30 euros, the refugees have to pay 35 to board. Little surcharges like these are nothing, of course, compared with the profiteering that the smugglers are engaging in: for each inflatable boat, which may have cost 2,000 or 3,000 euros, they collect well over 50,000, and they often cheat the refugees by selling more seats than there are, no matter how tightly the passengers are packed, so that they have to leave all their belongings behind.

Even the border guards can earn some extra cash by arbitrarily closing either the border or their eyes. This past summer the world was shocked by pictures of the border between Greece and Macedonia when refugees were driven back with clubs, tear gas, flash grenades and even gunshots. The local mafia took advantage of the situation, smuggling across the border those refugees who were able to pay. According to many accounts, the Macedonian authorities closed the border expressly to get a share of this business. Whether that is true or not, no official I talked to denies that the entire European asylum system is madness. But you also have to realize what the reason for the madness is: there is no other way for refugees to apply for asylum in Europe except by entering illegally. The European asylum agreements are nothing but a massive state aid programme for the human smuggling industry.

Yet it's not just the smugglers who benefit: it's also the right-wing populists, who exploit all the chaos at the borders to prophesy the imminent fall of Western civilization. Because they want to eradicate Europe's openness, the Hungarian and other nationalist governments reject the European Commission's proposals to create safe routes for the refugees and to distribute them among all the EU member states. In other words, those who rant the loudest against the chaos along the trail purposely promote the irregular mass migration by building fences, leaving refugees without sustenance, or dumping them outside their borders without consulting their neighbours, and often without registering their passage. In view of such outright selfishness, it strikes me as positively

➤ FOLLOWING PAGES:
Lesbos, Greece: a refugee who has just landed on a beach on the north coast waves to refugees aboard another inflatable boat.

unpatriotic for part of Germany's governing coalition to join forces with Victor Orbán himself, repudiating their own government's policy and the willingness of so many Germans to help. Instead of building fences too, we should be standing up for Europe. Only in cooperation and mutual assistance can Europe respond to this crisis, and I am referring not only to the admission of refugees but equally, if not more, to the causes of their flight: only a strong, united and liberal Europe can help the cause of peace in a world from which so many people are fleeing to our door.

It's true that there is no magic wand we could wave to make the refugee crisis vanish into thin air; war and poverty have advanced too close upon Europe, to say nothing of the other, deeper causes of flight, such as spreading aridity – primarily a consequence of climate change – which year after year destroys arable land totalling the area of Switzerland. Yet there have long been feasible proposals that would at least provide some control of the migrational movements and make them more manageable. One part of the solution which is overdue is to separate immigration and political asylum. But another is to extend the Geneva Refugee Convention by supplementary protocols to recognize conditions such as environmental degradation among the causes of flight. Immigration could be regulated according to the needs of the admitting countries while asylum remained available only to those in danger. That too would significantly reduce the pressure on Europe's external borders – which is necessary if they are to be secured again at all – since those who can hope to immigrate legally will invest their time and money, not in costly, dangerous clandestine travel, but in acquiring qualifications and language skills. Still more urgent is the need to support refugees closer to their home countries, in the camps around Syria and in northern Iraq for example, since many are waiting to return home, or would prefer to spend their exile surrounded by a familiar culture and language if the neighbouring countries offered any prospects at all. Rejecting or deporting people who are neither threatened nor have prospects of finding work is hard to accept – especially for a child of immigrants like myself – but would probably also be part of any realistic policy.

What is unrealistic, on the other hand – irrational in fact, since it has repeatedly been disproved by empirical evidence – is the notion that the refugee crisis could be solved by isolation. As long as there is virtually no chance of applying for legal immigration, and refugees cannot apply for asylum at any of Europe's external borders, both immigrants and refugees will continue to board the boats; and if Europe tries to stop them with military ships, as it did before, the boats will go back to using the longer, still more dangerous routes, hundreds of kilometres right across the Mediterranean Sea, or across the Atlantic to the Canary Islands. And immediately the news of the drownings will startle us again – two hundred here, six hundred there, several thousand dead every year at our borders – among them children, of course, whose pictures we will see in the news. We will never get this reality back out of our consciousness.

Heavy Seas

Landlocked Afghanistan now has its first seaport: Mytilene. At least today, most of the people on the promenade where the tourists ordinarily stroll up and down are Afghans; they too are in a holiday mood, one might think at first glance, the families among them the merriest because the laughing children make their parents laugh too. The eyes opened widest are those of the littlest children, sitting in their – bought, borrowed, donated? – pushchairs. Buy them an ice cream and they beam as children would anywhere in the world. Meanwhile the young men, freshly shaven, sit on the balustrade along the waterfront, their glossy hair styled after the fashion of our pro footballers and pop stars. Those in possession of a smartphone wiggle their feet up and down to the music. It's probably the first time since the beginning of their journey that these refugees have had time to catch their breath, to indulge their curiosity and look around in wonder: all the sailing boats, the yachts and, at the end of the harbour, the big ferry; all the boutiques, restaurants and stylish cafés. Very few of them can afford a hotel, but by now they're all accustomed to sleeping in the street. A tent costs 30 euros, a sleeping bag 10, a roll mat 5 to make the asphalt more bearable; the souvenir shops of Mytilene – those that have added camping gear to their assortment – are still doing a modest business.

The restaurants and cafés on the other hand are mostly empty: what Afghan can afford 3 euros for a cappuccino, when an Afghan doctor earns 3 euros a day? *No charge phones, no wifi, no toilet* is written on A4-sized signs on nearly every door and shop window, even on the kiosks. It is hard to blame the inhabitants if a welcoming culture is not exactly prevalent: since the tourists are staying away, they have lost their most important source of revenue. On the contrary, I am surprised how many locals show friendly faces and gestures nonetheless. Here and there a couple sits at a table and wonders in turn at all the exotic faces going by, Arabs of course in addition to the Afghans, but also Bangladeshis, Tamils and scattered sub-Saharan

➤ FOLLOWING PAGES:
*Lesbos, Greece: refugees disembarking from the inflatable boat
that brought them over from Assos, Turkey.*

Africans, the women dressed in vibrant colours. In Mytilene the refugees are enjoying their first taste of peace. Waiting here for a place on the ferry to Piraeus is not a time of uncertainty and fear like the other stages of their journey up to now, but one of relief and hope.

We buy a ferry ticket ourselves, but for a smaller ship, and in the opposite direction, to Ayvalık on the Turkish coast. To cross the neck of water that costs the refugees a fortune, heart palpitations, and possibly their lives, we pay a few euros and look forward to drinking tea on deck in the afternoon sun. The port of Mytilene has been transformed into an outdoor hostel, with freight containers here and there as blinds, the sea as a pool for the young people and the ubiquitous portable toilets. Through an inconspicuous door that remains closed to the refugees, although the reasons for their journey are so much more urgent, we enter the ferry terminal for the regular passport check. It takes no longer than a glance at our IDs and our faces. As humanity was once divided into different hereditary ranks, today it is citizenship and residence rights that create first, second and third-class persons – it is hard for a Western European of today to understand what borders mean to a citizen of an impoverished or ostracized state, to say nothing of a stateless person or a refugee.

We leave the building at the rear and find ourselves in a fenced-off, clean, almost empty section of the port. Lined up in a row in front of our ship are the little outboard motors that the pickup trucks have collected on the north coast, dozens, hundreds of them: no wonder we hear again and again about motors failing in the open water if the smugglers are selling the same ones over and over. Not until our little ship sails out of the harbour do we get a clear view of the giant ferry at the other end of the quay. It reminds me, though perhaps only because I have met so many refugees, of a whale, the narrow upper deck like a fin, the funnel a blowhole, the open doors a wide open mouth. Or would any Bible reader make the same association? Most would probably be reminded rather of Noah's ark, especially since a long, seemingly endless queue of refugees has formed, although the ferry doesn't sail until midnight. Unlike Jonah, they can hardly wait to be admitted into its belly.

The crossing is supposed to take just an hour and a half, so I lean back and close my eyes to enjoy the sea air, the gentle rocking and the warmth of the sun's last rays. When I wake up I'm alone on deck. What was a pleasant breeze on shore is a cold gale on the open sea; I have to lean into it to take a step forward. The gentle waves have grown into a swell that sprays water fifteen feet up onto the deck. To get at least

---

➢ FOLLOWING PAGES:
Lesbos, Greece: Syrian refugees who have just landed on the north coast.

some idea, however inadequate, of how the refugees feel crossing this sea in their low inflatable boats, I climb down the stairs and go forward hand over hand along the rail. When I get to the bow, the ship is rising so high on each wave before crashing down again that I have to hold on with both hands. After the first second, I am wet from head to toe and the wind feels icy on my skin. And the refugees are separated from the water only by a thin plastic sheet, and sit so close together that they can only cling to the back of the person in front of them to keep from falling overboard. The shorter route to the north coast takes them three hours, even in ideal weather, much longer in heavy seas, or even days if the motor fails. I have seen their faces, relieved at last or still panic-stricken, when the rubber boats land on the north coast of Lesbos; I can still hear their cries of jubilation and their convulsive sobbing. It's no wonder after all that the refugees would go willingly into the belly of a whale.

Human Instinct

Facing the north coast of Lesbos is the ancient city of Assos, now a picturesque fishing village in Turkey with a few charming hotels and restaurants. The sparsely populated strip of coastline around Assos is where most of the refugees who walked past my hotel veranda boarded the boats. Sitting by the roadside a few hundred yards beyond the amphitheatre is a young man who turns out to be a Syrian Kurd. His name is Muhammad. 'The boat was so full,' he says in good English, 'that I panicked and jumped back at the last minute.'

Muhammad was studying business administration in Hfasakah in northeastern Syria until the city was conquered by IS. On the twentieth of March he saw a car bomb explode at close range, killing twenty-six people, saw the body parts flying, heard screams as loud as a woman in childbirth and smelled the biting stench of burnt flesh – still has dreams about it. Taken in by relatives in a neighbouring town that was not yet controlled by IS, he applied to a German university. He mentions that his grades were among the best in his class, not to boast, but to explain why he had hopes of travelling to Germany legally – and besides, he's more the overcautious type. When he had received no answer six months later, and in spite of his inquiries, not even an acknowledgement that his application had been received, he overcame his fear and flew to Beirut last week – it is almost impossible now, Muhammad reports, to get to Turkey directly from northern Syria, although in the opposite direction

➤ FOLLOWING PAGES:
Lesbos, Greece: a father comforts his daughter after they have reached the coast aboard an inflatable boat.

Turkey continues to let jihadists through – and from Beirut to Istanbul. From Istanbul he took a bus to Izmir, where he met the smuggler.

'No one wants peace for Syria,' says Muhammad; 'IS is there to stay, Assad is there to stay, no one in the world is challenging them.'

Yesterday evening at eleven he was driven in a car to a wooded plot of land near Assos where some other Syrians had already gathered. Hardly any of them slept for excitement and cold; the refugees sat leaning against trees without talking. From daybreak on, they observed the ships of the Turkish coastguard, counted how many of the other boats were intercepted – at least every other one, Muhammad remembers. When they finally spotted a gap in the patrols, everything went very fast. Everyone jumped in the boat, and he too was already standing in the water when his nerves got the better of him.

'It's all right,' Muhammad says, 'I'll try again.'

Fortunately, his 1,200 euros are not lost; the refugees usually deposit the money with an agency and give the smugglers the code to collect it only after they have landed. Muhammad will work illegally in a textile factory for a few months to earn the 800 dollars more for a seat in a wooden boat. His friends from Izmir are already on the way to fetch him in Assos. 'It's all right,' Muhammad assures me once more, and points to a track leading into the woods: 'Go that way if you want to see the people who are really hard up. But watch out for the smugglers.'

Where the track meets the road, three men are sitting on a rock who look like some of those Muhammad was talking about. They are in their mid- to late twenties, not villagers like most of the refugees; back home in Kabul or Kunduz they dreamt of the free West. They worked for four months on building sites in Istanbul, twelve, sixteen hours a day, seven days a week, to earn the money for the smuggler, went to Izmir and booked the boat trip. The day before yesterday they were finally brought to the woods near Assos, but there was no boat for them, only Turks with guns drawn who forced them to hand over their code.

'That means the money ...?'

'Gone.'

They haven't eaten since yesterday, they're parched with thirst, and now they can't go on and can't go back. Somehow they have to make it to Istanbul or another big city, find some kind of work, but how can an Afghan do that without a lira in his pocket, with no belongings, with no warm clothes? If only the police would pick them up.

'It was a mistake to leave Afghanistan,' one of the men says forcefully; 'there was war there, but at least we had a roof over our heads: we shouldn't have left.'

'Yes, we imagined it all wrong,' another agrees.

With the money, when they earn it, they don't want to pay another boat fare, but to go back to Afghanistan, or try their luck in Iran, where people at least speak their language.

'But in Iran they hate us too,' the third Afghan objects.

I ask where the track leads.

'That way you'll find the people who haven't eaten for five days.'

We go along the track and meet five Afghans, barely twenty years old, if that, who say they mustn't say anything, and yet reveal at least this much: their boat didn't come either. They had to disclose their code anyway. When I ask another question, they run away. Then an old white estate car comes past us with three men inside, looking at us in surprise. At least they don't threaten us. Because the track appears to be passable, we go back to get our car too. As we drive in, we pass the estate car coming back. A few minutes later the path is blocked by another car whose driver is sleeping with his mouth wide open. We get out and find ourselves directly above the wooded plot, which looks like a scene from Hell in the middle of a heavenly natural landscape: covered in rubbish, with dozens or hundreds of people lying under the trees or dragging themselves from one spot to another. We watch the boats setting out from the wood every few minutes, even though the coastguard cutters are patrolling offshore. Maybe it's last-minute panic, or else they're trying to overwhelm the coastguard with so many boats in rapid succession. One boat is surrounded by four cutters; the rest seem to be getting across to Lesbos.

In some bushes we discover the five Afghans who ran away from us an hour ago. They have three bottles of water which they have nearly finished, and there are two empty tins on the ground. Apparently the estate car brought them some provisions, their first meal in days, the Afghans confirm: white beans in tomato sauce, which they slurped down cold, I assume; there are no spoons in sight. The question as to who the men in the estate car were draws no answer but prompts them to disappear again, down a steep path that seems to lead into the woods. No, we shouldn't come with them; the guards have knives and guns. One of the Afghans goes to drink another mouthful of water before they leave, and – unconsciously no doubt, driven by a yet unwithered instinct – he performs a gesture that is at least as mad as the whole European border regime: although the little bit of water that is left has to last him who knows how many days, he offers me the bottle first.

Zero Refugees Here

Our hired car struggles backwards along the narrow, bumpy track until we finally find a place to turn around. When we reach the road, we turn, not right down the hill towards Assos, but left, then left again at the dual carriageway, and left once more at the first junction until we have gone all the way around the hill to the sea. On the long, otherwise deserted beach are a couple embracing and a squad of police in a loose formation, twenty-five or thirty officers in immaculate blue uniforms. They seem to be waiting for their next operation. I hail their commander, who greets me affably in reply, and introduce myself as a reporter from Germany. He explains in quite fluent English that his squad are guarding this section of the coastline.

'Because of the refugees?' I ask.

'Yes, because of the refugees,' the officer answers.

'Do any get through?'

'No, no one gets through here.'

'But I saw some get through.'

'You must be mistaken. You see those ships out there, those are all coastguard ships.'

When I try to report what I saw from the hilltop, the officer explains in suddenly broken English that he doesn't understand me, he is sorry but he only speaks Turkish. Besides, he has to get back to his men. 'Here no refugees,' he declares categorically, and takes his leave: 'Excuse me.'

I follow him and point to the wooded hill jutting into the sea two, three kilometres eastwards. There are refugees there; they have been there practically without supplies for the past several days or maybe even weeks, apparently being bullied by smugglers. The officer shakes his head and apologizes again that his English is not good enough to understand me.

'There!' I cry, pointing again with my finger at the hill. 'Many refugees there!'

'No refugees here,' the policeman affirms, and shows me the palms of his hands, moving them alternately together and apart like windscreen wipers: 'Zero refugees here.'

Bargaining for Their Lives

Across from Basmane Gar, the main railway station of Izmir, is the tea house where the refugees bargain for their lives. After all, their whole future depends on whether the smuggler they put their trust in is honest.

➤ FOLLOWING PAGES:
Assos, Turkey: the three Afghans by the wayside who tell of being cheated out of their passage by smugglers.

To be exact, the person who solicits the refugees' business is only an agent, someone who speaks their language; that makes it harder still for the refugees to make the right choice, since even the agent may not know the head of the outfit personally. It's eight in the morning and the first negotiations have already begun: just two tables away a Syrian family sit on either side of a middle-aged man who taps again and again on his smartphone and holds the display up to the customers – prices for different routes, I assume, for different boats. The family have their baggage with them, a compact but overfilled sports holdall each; they are two men and a woman of about thirty and a boy perhaps five years old, a plush kangaroo sticking out of his rucksack. The two men, who may be brothers or brothers-in-law, are either playing good cop, bad cop, or they are really in disagreement as to whether they should accept the offer. While one of them asks a question, the other sceptically shakes his head and turns away. The agent tries hard to lighten the gravity of the conversation, smiles a lot and banters with the woman. His youthful outfit also signals nonchalance: trainers, a hooded sweatshirt and a black rain jacket with three fluorescent green stripes. The woman, who apparently is in the biggest hurry, ostentatiously echoes his cheerful, optimistic tone. Maybe she's doing so for her son's sake, trying to soothe his fears. I don't know what results the talks have achieved when the agent pays for the tea and leaves the tea house with the family. Refugees always have their baggage with them.

Chancellor Merkel's Shoe

Also at Basmane Gar, the station radiating an Oriental early modern flair between the multi-lane roads and faceless city blocks, is an Ottoman mosque. I suspect I'll find refugees there – in Islam too, after all, houses of worship have always offered sanctuary to strangers – but I find the gates locked. I follow the fence around to a side street and find a back entrance leading to a little courtyard and the washhouse. This is where the refugees are living: not in the mosque, but in the open air; not on the soft carpet, but on bare stone. There are about a dozen families, with children and old people, who have run out of money. They have pushed their baggage and their rolled-up plastic mats to one side and are sitting in little groups on the ground or on the chairs of the tea room attached to the mosque. Striking up a conversation with them is easy; they have so much time and so much to tell.

One family lived through the Syrian regime's massacres in Daraa, at the southern end of Syria, in 2011 and 2012; another lost all hope of peace in Deir ez-Zor, a city on the Euphrates heavily disputed between IS and Syrian troops. Surrounded by their children, for whom I seem to be quite simply a passing amusement, I sit on a folded blanket of heavy wool and gradually lose track of whose story is whose. The stories are not only about their homes in Syria and Iraq but also about oppression and war, about flight and how they ran out of money, lost it or had it stolen. 'Where can we go?' they all ask, and are afraid in the end they might have to go back to choose between two deaths, the one administered by the regime or the one dispensed by the 'Islamic State'.

'We need to learn to walk across the water like Jesus,' one father scoffs, an English teacher from Damascus who is now the children's schoolteacher in the courtyard of the mosque.

'Is there no Arab country you can go to?' I ask.

'We came here from Jordan,' another father chimes in, and reports that refugees there do not receive work permits, there are simply too many of them now: 1.4 million according to the official figures. That's as much as 20 per cent of the Jordanian population. And the United Nations refugee agency had to cut its already modest aid this year because the international donor countries have not disbursed the funds they promised. 'Are we supposed to live as beggars?'

the father continues, 'Will my children have to grow up in a tent?'

'And the Gulf states?'

'The Gulf states!' he laughs, as if I had made a joke. 'The Emirates charge 6,000 dollars just for the visa.'

'Germany respects human rights, that's the most important thing,' adds a woman, wearing a headscarf like all the women in the mosque's courtyard.

'Chancellor Merkel's shoe is worth more than all the Arab leaders,' her husband exclaims.

'Her shoe?'

'Yes, her shoe,' says the man, and has to chuckle himself.

'I'll pay attention to her shoes next time I see Chancellor Merkel on television.'

'Yes, do that, pay attention to her shoes, and remember my words: each of her shoes is worth more than all the Arab leaders together.'

'And the pair is worth more than the Arab world!' the English teacher agrees.

Laughing is a way of asserting their humanity in spite of the abyss that gapes before and behind them. 'The sole of her shoe,' they chortle, and then: 'The dirt under the sole of the chancellor's shoe is worth more than the whole Arab world.' And it is not only laughter that is a means of self-affirmation; so are the school instruction they give their children, the clean-swept courtyard, the conspicuously well-kept clothes, and the repeated references to the professions they exercised, the qualifications they have. Perhaps because they feel abandoned by the world – and they practically are – their will is strong, as the will of refugees has always been, not to abandon themselves. And yet the most mundane concern stings them: that they have to pay a lira, the equivalent of 30 cents, every time they go to the toilet. There are no portable toilets at Basmane Gar.

'And after evening prayers, the washhouse is closed,' a lean old man complains. 'Beg as we may, the caretaker doesn't even let the women, or even the sick children, use the toilet.'

He is alone, the only one here on his own, the old man says; he was the head of a tiny village in Syria and got separated from his people just after they'd crossed the Turkish border, he doesn't know exactly where, when the police seized them in the middle of a huge crowd of refugees and divided them up into different buses. He had had very little money and no telephone with him to find his family again, and so he made his way to Izmir, on foot, by bus and hitchhiking, in the hope of meeting them near Basmane Gar. Taking responsibility is in his blood somehow; he has practically become the speaker of the families living by the washhouse of the Basmane mosque, and a few nights ago he couldn't stand it any more, and cried out first to the caretaker, then to the imam, and finally to God to let the women go to the toilet. The men can duck around a corner somewhere, he says; but a woman, who may have her period, or a child with diarrhoea – where are they supposed to go in the middle of the city when even the tea houses are closed?

'Is there no one helping you?' I ask, 'some organization, the Turkish state, the United Nations, anybody?'

'Once a week a team of doctors comes by and gives out medicines,' the old man answers, 'that's all.'

'And what do you live on?'

'We live on the kindness of our neighbours,' says the old man, and tells how the inhabitants and the merchants of the neighbourhood supply the refugees with clothes, blankets, daily food, and a few lira for the neediest. For the mosque takes money, not just for the use of bathroom and toilet, but for charging phones and for every glass of tea. 'I am a devout man, I never miss prayers. But an Islam that knows no compassion is not worth an excrement.'

You Can Live without Freedom

Turkey has admitted over two million refugees, and so Arabic has become the second language in the lanes of the quarter around Basmane Gar. Many people carry compact sports holdalls or overfilled rucksacks, and they walk more slowly than ordinary city-dwellers or take endless time over a single tea in front of the cafés, sitting for hours after their glass has been cleared away. Apparently no one drives them from their seats. Now, with so many Syrians living in Izmir, some of the tea houses also offer hookahs, which are not otherwise common in Turkey. In the cheap guesthouses that are found in every street, a single room costs about 10 euros; rooms with several beds or dormitories are cheaper. You can also hire by the hour if you just want to lie on a mattress again. Those who have more money or know they'll stay longer take furnished flats, which are advertised on notices posted everywhere. The snack bars are flourishing because, although very few refugees can afford a restaurant, they all have to eat something; likewise the Internet cafés, bureaux de change, money transfer offices, hair stylists, barbers, and public baths. The best sellers are the life vests, blazing red and orange in the windows of the clothing shops.

In one of these shops offering equipment for a sea voyage between the shirts and jeans, I claim to be from Iran. The young shop assistant, himself a Syrian, has apparently never met a German who speaks Arabic, otherwise he would have placed my accent.

But I don't have to invent any elaborate cover story to persuade him that I am a writer and that writers have a very hard time of it in Iran; that's no lie.

'Are you on your own?' the shop assistant asks.

'Yes,' I reply, 'I'll send for my family when I get there.'

'God willing,' the assistant nods; he doesn't have to ask what I mean by 'there'.

Then he asks – we haven't exchanged ten sentences since I walked into the shop – whether he can put me in touch with a trustworthy smuggler: one phone call and a man will be there in twenty minutes.

Over the tea the shop assistant brings me, I ask him about the prices of the various life vests, the types of boats and the different Greek islands. He seems quite knowledgeable, I must say, although his persistent use of the word 'yacht' for the wooden tubs that cost 800 euros more to board than the inflatable boats strikes me as a bit cynical. Apart from that, he understates neither the duration nor the dangers of the crossing, and he also mentions the long march on foot that awaits me on Lesbos, advising me for that reason to choose the route from Bodrum to Kos. I have heard so many refugees – especially Afghans – complain about smugglers who promised them the world, a one-hour pleasure cruise and then a European Union welcome centre right in the Greek port. Although he will certainly get a commission, and as a Syrian is probably employed in this shop in the first place mainly to introduce his countrymen to the smuggler, the assistant does not sugar-coat the refugee's journey. Instead, he asks why I want to escape from Iran at all; there's no war in Iran.

'That's true,' I reply, 'but there's no freedom.'

'Believe me,' says the young Syrian, who in the course of the revolution has lost his country, 'you can live without freedom, but not without peace.'

I ask him what he thinks of many Europeans' concern that there are jihadists travelling among the refugees. That is an issue of great concern among the Syrians, the shop assistant says; everyone here has had bad experiences with IS and is afraid of their spies. For his part, he thinks it's absurd because IS has enough money to smuggle attackers to Europe more quickly, safely and comfortably than in inflatable boats. On the other hand, though, he has seen the jihadists himself.

'You've seen them?' I ask.

'Yes, on Facebook,' the shop assistant replies, and takes out his smartphone to show me two photos of a bearded man, one taken evidently in Syria or Iraq, the other in the front yard of a terraced house somewhere in Western Europe. The man in the first photo is wearing a jellabiya and holding up two severed heads;

the man in the second photo is wearing Western street clothes and holding two smiling children by the hand.

'Are you sure it's the same man?'

'That's what it says in the caption, and look: they both have the same grin.'

Both men are grinning, it's true, but the faces are too small on the phone's display, the beards are too thick, for anyone to say with certainty that it's the same grin. Photos like this, quickly put together, get viral distribution on Facebook. What the Europeans find troubling is positively frightening to the refugees.

Go Back?

I come to the square in front of the Hatuniye mosque, where the trees offer a pleasant shade and many of the surrounding buildings still have ornate grilles on the old wooden bay windows. Pedlars have spread blankets on the ground on which they present second-hand clothing, watertight bags for smartphones, and toiletries. Several families have tied sheets of cloth slanting down from the bars on the mosque so that they can crawl under them to sleep or to change their clothes. There are chairs not just in front of the tea houses but scattered all over the square. Whoever put them there, inhabitants and refugees alike are glad, and they sit, in silence or talking in small groups, without having to pay a lira for a glass of tea. The scene looks remarkably tranquil, and indeed I am surprised to have seen generally, in spite of the refugees' hardships and psychological stress, few instances of aggression or even raised voices. The only fight I saw took place on Lesbos, and that was between an aid worker and a photographer. I suspect it is because of their uncertain status, their dependence on help and acceptance, that many refugees take pains to look neat, that they are friendly, show their gratitude, and avoid anything that could classify them as an additional burden. At the same time, I may have been biased by my reading: German literature has given particular attention to describing the psychology of refugees, Joseph Roth no less than Bertolt Brecht, and more recently Herta Müller. As different as their reasons for fleeing may be, the effects on their psyche are probably the same: the hopes and fears, the shame and the anxiousness to please, and also the depression or anger when, even if they reach their destination, they find no future there. And perhaps their reasons aren't so different after all.

I sit down on an empty chair and wonder what story the stoutish, rather unkempt-looking man beside me might have: unshaven, the long hair at the sides laid carelessly across his bald head, not just his shirt spotty, but his brown suit shabby, with holes in some places.

'Where from?' I ask.

'Mosul,' the man answers, looking at me out of dark, unbelievably sad eyes that look like sewn-on buttons in his round face. I don't need to ask again to learn his story. His name is Muhammad Yusuf Zaidan, he is fifty-six years old, and he owned a whole chain of shops in Mosul. But in Mosul you can't smoke, you can't go out with your wife, you can't work, and if you work, you have to finance IS with what you earn.

'Is there really no one at all in Mosul who is happy about IS?' I ask.

'They are animals,' says Mr Zaidan. 'What human being is happy when he is ruled by animals?'

'But IS must have supporters too.'

'You have no idea what's going on in Mosul. It's terror, day after day. Some are perpetrating it, all the others are being terrorized. Why do you think I'm here? I had everything there, a family, a house, two cars; I was somebody. Now I'm nobody.'

Muhammad Yusuf Zaidan sewed a large part of his money, cash worth 45,000 euros, into the lining of his coat and fled Mosul eighteen days ago. He left his family behind because he thought the road would be too dangerous, especially the Islamic State's check-points. More by luck than judgement, he made it to

---

➤ FOLLOWING PAGES:
Belgrade, Serbia: the feet of a refugee sleeping in a park
near the central railway station.

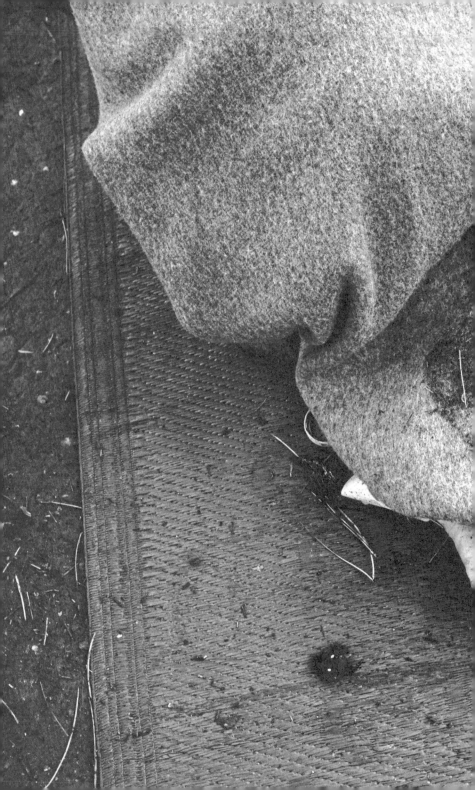

Turkey, exhausted by long marches on foot, but safe and sound, only to be beaten senseless by several men on the first evening. Mr Zaidan turns his suit coat inside out and shows me where the lining has been ripped open. The robbers took his bag too, his smart-phone, his ID, and so on.

'And now?' I ask.

'The way back is even more dangerous,' Mr Zaidan replies.

Just in Time

When the train arrives in Cologne on the evening of 6 December 2015, the refugees stay in their seats, uncertain, staring at the platform. Aid workers in blue safety vests and interpreters in green ones must first walk down the corridor, calling into the compartments, before the refugees pack up their belongings and leave the train. There are fewer than two hundred of them, instead of the four hundred and sixty that were announced this morning, and there is only one train coming today instead of the usual two. The many empty seats stand for the latest obstacles that now dot the route to Europe: the sea of course, which has grown stormy, and also Turkey's more determined surveillance of its coastline, which the European Union has instigated by paying a great deal of money and kowtowing to the Erdoğan government. Furthermore, the Balkan states now wave through only Iraqis, Syrians and Afghans, so that all other refugees are either stranded at the borders or pay still more money to smugglers.

But the ones sitting in this train have made it just in time – before the onset of winter and the complete closing of the borders. They boarded the train this morning in Passau on the border between Germany and Austria, and apparently they don't know they're in Cologne now; in any case they ask where they are as soon as they get off the train, and then they ask where Cologne is – but it's in Germany, that's all that matters. It's odd that only families are stepping out onto the windy platform at the Cologne airport railway station, many children, many women, many old people. Have the young single men been stopped at the border too, or are they merely, having arrived in Germany, now making their own way to their destinations? The administrative staff from the city of Cologne, identified by red safety vests, would like to know that too. Communication with Passau could be improved, one official says politely; even the number of refugees coming is announced at very short notice.

That is why today there are almost too many helpers waiting for the refugees on the platform and in the tents as big as sports halls – at least one to one from the looks of it. The refugees rub their eyes at the many hands carrying their luggage and their small children, the words of welcome and the friendly faces everywhere. The staff managing the clothing supplies, who are also volunteers, recognizable by their grey vests, are noting right on the platform who needs a jacket, a jumper, trousers or shoes, writing down the sizes on their lists. Paramedics, strong soldiers from the barracks in nearby Porz, and no fewer than five doctors offer their help – all of them here outside their regular shifts. And how many Germans speak the refugees' languages! For not only the interpreters but also the other volunteers and even the city employees include a disproportionate number of children of Arab, Kurdish, Persian and Afghan immigrants. Perhaps they have been given this assignment preferentially; after all, more than enough citizens in Germany are volunteering, even so close to the holidays. A caller to Cologne city hall volunteering to help at the 'refugee hub' ends up on a long waiting list, and, even if he knows Persian and Arabic, he is assured for the time being that everyone gets their turn, but his will be in three or four weeks at the earliest.

The 'hub', so called because the refugees are distributed from here, after two or three hours, to reception camps elsewhere in North Rhine-Westphalia, is the camp on the vacant ground between the airport's railway station and the number 2 car park. The tents are heated and have wooden flooring, and even such decorations as circumstances allow: pictures drawn by Cologne schoolchildren, screens displaying basic information and a big poster welcoming the refugees. The procedure is impressively well organized by the authorities and the aid workers, all of whom are volunteers. Even before the refugees arrive, fruit, chocolate and water are ready on the folding tables, and they have no sooner sat down than they are served soup and tea. The wireless Internet access is free, so they can quickly notify their relatives; enough power sockets are available to charge phones, and the children quickly make friends with the volunteers assigned to the play corner. There is a cashier to exchange money, a changing room for babies, a prayer niche, and ticket vending machines for those who are making their own further travel arrangements. The helpers standing by the vending machines are connected by phone with other volunteers at home who can search on their computers for the cheapest connections. Guides are also on hand to escort the refugees to Cologne's main station, where trains depart for the rest of Germany or for Scandinavia.

It takes a moment for the refugees to get settled, but after a while the tension dissolves and the atmosphere in the tent becomes quite cheerful. Especially today, as not all the volunteers are busy, long, sometimes emotional conversations take place at the tables – or, if not conversations, then amiable looks and sympathetic gestures, as the refugees can't express their gratitude often enough. And, at the same time, there is something unreal about the scene, not just to the refugees, who are experiencing such a friendly, empathetic reception for the first time on their arduous journey, and probably wondering whether this Germany will still be as full of brotherly love tomorrow morning. The helpers are wondering the same thing.

For today, the sixth of December, the Front national are emerging as the triumphant winners of the regional elections in France, and in Germany's next largest neighbour, Poland, the new government has openly proclaimed its commitment to Victor Orbán's Europe, in which there is no room for refugees. Other Eastern European states, and even the president of the European Council, have also expressed vehement opposition to the German refugee policy. And in Germany itself, the right-wing populists are gaining support, and Angela Merkel is being pressured to change course by members of her own party. The head of the Bavarian state government, who gave Victor Orbán an ostentatiously friendly reception in late September, showed a complete lack of courtesy when his own chancellor was invited to his party's convention. The number of attacks on refugee shelters is increasing dramatically – to 817 so far this year, according to the federal police. Yet the federal government has long since stepped up its efforts to reduce the number of refugees: made the asylum laws harsher; restricted reunion visas, which were rarely granted to begin with; begun planning transit zones; called desperately at summit meetings for a European border defence. But a common refugee policy such as the European Commission is trying to develop has been set back a long way by the recent and the expected future electoral successes of nationalist parties. Even liberal Sweden, which admits the most refugees of all European countries in proportion to its population, has reintroduced border checks, and, in Germany, even Green local politicians say we have reached the breaking point. The attacks of 13 November in Paris, which killed 130 people, have added fresh fuel to Islamophobia, and the fact that two of the perpetrators apparently entered as refugees confirms people's worst fears. The air war in Syria, in which the larger European states have been participating since then, will undoubtedly be more effective in driving still more people to flee than in combating the 'Islamic State'.

For all Germany's spectacular celebration of 'welcoming culture' in September, three months later the country collectively seems to feel exhausted – at least, if we believe that segment of the press that is now counterbalancing its initial proclamation of hospitality with all the more strident warnings. But perhaps the German media's euphoria was just as posed and exaggerated as their present displeasure. The public willingness to help, in any case, has not abated, as authorities everywhere confirm, and as the scene at Cologne airport's railway station demonstrates. And once it has been deeply moved, touched by real encounters with human beings, Germany will not so easily forget the distress and the gratitude of the refugees. In Cologne too, as at every stage of the refugees' route, it is mostly young people who have volunteered, twenty, twenty-five-year-olds, and with so many different cultures, skills, languages, as if all of them together were the incarnation of the European idea. If so, they will preserve and renew the Europe that our generation, no longer scarred by war and fascism, is threatening to throw away.

Map

FINLAND

ESTONIA

LATVIA

SWEDEN

*Baltic
Sea*

LITHUANIA

DENMARK

POLAND

GERMANY

CZECH
REP.

SLOVAKIA

●**Cologne**

Budapest

HUNGARY

AUSTRIA

Black Sea

ROMANIA

LUXEMBOURG

SLOVENIA

SERBIA

Opatovac
Šid

●**Belgrade**

BULGARIA

●**Istanbul**

●**Ank**

CROATIA

Preševo
Miratovac

Tabanovce

TURKEY

FRANCE

ITALY

Gevgelija

Idomeni

Lesbos

Assos

Izmir

Piraeus

GREECE

CY

Mediterranean Sea

MALTA

●**Tunis**

●**Algiers**

●**Tripoli**

SERBIA

Obrovac ○

Opatovac ○

Bačka Palanka ○

CROATIA

Ilok ○

Tovarnik ○

Šid ○

SERBIA

0   5 km

⬭ Member states of the European Union